IT'S TIME TO EAT HONEYDEW MELONS

It's Time to Eat HONEYDEW MELONS

Walter the Educator

Silent King Books
A WhichHead Entertainment Imprint

Copyright © 2024 by Walter the Educator

All rights reserved. No part of this book may be reproduced in any manner whatsoever without written per- mission except in the case of brief quotations embodied in critical articles and reviews.

First Printing, 2024

Disclaimer

This book is a literary work; the story is not about specific persons, locations, situations, and/or circumstances unless mentioned in a historical context. Any resemblance to real persons, locations, situations, and/or circumstances is coincidental. This book is for entertainment and informational purposes only. The author and publisher offer this information without warranties expressed or implied. No matter the grounds, neither the author nor the publisher will be accountable for any losses, injuries, or other damages caused by the reader's use of this book. The use of this book acknowledges an understanding and acceptance of this disclaimer.

It's Time to Eat HONEYDEW MELONS is a collectible early learning book by Walter the Educator suitable for all ages belonging to Walter the Educator's Time to Eat Book Series. Collect more books at WaltertheEducator.com

USE THE EXTRA SPACE TO TAKE NOTES AND DOCUMENT YOUR MEMORIES

HONEYDEW MELONS

It's time to eat, the moment's here,

It's Time to Eat
Honeydew Melons

The honeydew's ripe, sweet and clear!

Its skin so smooth, a gentle green,

The tastiest fruit you've ever seen.

A slice of joy, so fresh and sweet,

A perfect summer snack to eat.

Soft and juicy, cool and light,

A melon treat that feels just right.

Take a bite and taste the sun,

Eating honeydew is so much fun!

Its flavor dances, soft and mild,

Nature's candy, pure and wild.

Chop it up in little squares,

Share with friends, and show who cares.

A plate of melon, bright and round,

Happiness in every mound!

It's Time to Eat
Honeydew Melons

Pack it up for lunch today,

Honeydew makes work feel like play.

In a picnic, bowl, or on the go,

Its sweetness follows where you go.

It's healthy, too, for you and me,

A fruit as good as it can be!

Packed with water, vitamins too,

A bite of health in honeydew.

Mix it up in fruit-filled bowls,

Melons, berries, tasty goals!

Add some mint, a drizzle of lime,

A recipe for a snack sublime.

The bees once buzzed to help it grow,

The farmer's care made sweetness show.

Now it's here, for you to taste,

It's Time to Eat
Honeydew Melons

Not a single bite should go to waste!

So grab a slice, let's shout hooray,

For honeydew on this fine day.

The perfect treat, so fresh and true,

Hooray, hooray for honeydew!

When you're done, remember well,

Save the seeds, so you can tell,

Honeydew will grow again,

It's Time to Eat Honeydew Melons

And bring us joy, just like a friend!

ABOUT THE CREATOR

Walter the Educator is one of the pseudonyms for Walter Anderson. Formally educated in Chemistry, Business, and Education, he is an educator, an author, a diverse entrepreneur, and he is the son of a disabled war veteran. "Walter the Educator" shares his time between educating and creating. He holds interests and owns several creative projects that entertain, enlighten, enhance, and educate, hoping to inspire and motivate you. Follow, find new works, and stay up to date with Walter the Educator™

at WaltertheEducator.com

www.ingramcontent.com/pod-product-compliance
Lightning Source LLC
LaVergne TN
LVHW051921060526
838201LV00060B/4116